John H. Johnson

Business Leader

by Eileen Bromley
illustrated by Charles Shaw

D0166754

HOUGHTON MIFFLIN   BOSTON

John H. Johnson's mother taught him to work hard. She told him to believe in himself.

2

John decided to start a magazine for African Americans when he was a young man. There weren't many stories about African Americans in newspapers and magazines at that time.

Some people told John that no one would buy his magazine.

John did not listen. He believed in his idea.

John's mother used the services of a bank to help him get a loan. He wrote letters to tell people about his idea.

John's magazine, *Negro Digest*, went on
sale in November 1942. It was a big hit. Now
he had his own magazine business.

John H. Johnson also made many other
magazines for African Americans. He is now
well known as a business leader.